The Beatitudes

The Pathway to Discipleship

Michael L. D'Spain

WESTBOW
PRESS®
A DIVISION OF THOMAS NELSON
& ZONDERVAN

WestBow Press books may be ordered through booksellers or by contacting:

WestBow Press
A Division of Thomas Nelson & Zondervan
1663 Liberty Drive
Bloomington, IN 47403
www.westbowpress.com
1 (866) 928-1240

ISBN: 978-1-4908-9913-8 (sc)
ISBN: 978-1-4908-9914-5 (e)

Print information available on the last page.

WestBow Press rev. date: 01/15/2016

Contents

Foreword

Thirty years ago I met a young Air Force officer in Seattle, Washington. He was a student at the University of Washington, earning his Masters Degree in Meteorology while serving in the military and raising his family. His beautiful wife, Gail, and their two sons (they had their third son a few years later) attended our church, and that's how we met. I was a Christian counselor and Bible teacher.

Michael and I began to study the scriptures together once or twice a week. We prayed about the important things in our lives and Mike shared with me about his young family. He told wonderful, funny stories about David and Adam, and about all the things that can go wrong when you're raising boys!

Over the years Mike has grown in his understanding of how God works in our lives. He has taught the Bible in church and home bible studies, and he has shared his faith with countless people.

It is unspeakably wonderful that, all these years after we met, Michael has written a book that incorporates his love for the Lord Jesus, and the Bible, his humor, and the wisdom and experience he has gained as the father of three sons.

This study of the Beatitudes is different from other similar studies because the heart and soul of the author leaps off the pages to touch your life. In these pages you will gain a new insight into the words of the Savior through the eyes and the life of a Godly man and father, according to the light he has received from God's Word. Mike's insight will help you apply the truths of the Beatitudes to your own life.

So sit back, relax and prepare to smile. This book will touch your heart and change your life.

Rev. Lou Carlson
Santa Ana, CA

Preface

Have you wondered, as I have, about the words from Jesus in Matthew 4:3-12? We know they are important; they just seem out of place. They are beautiful bullet points of thought stuck into His discourse. Many times we look at each verse separately, losing sight of the bigger picture.

Sermons seem to take each verse as separate and distinct thoughts that just happen to always be presented together. We realize they are important characteristics of a disciple; we just have difficulty tying them together. Jesus spends the remaining time of His discourse explaining the change in perspective from the external law to the internal condition of the heart.

Jesus was a Jewish rabbi. We have the advantage of looking back into history and acknowledging Him as the Son of God, the Messiah, the Savior of the world, but to the Jews of that time He was a rabbi. Disciples were chosen by a rabbi to essentially live with the rabbi and become his students. The disciples would not just learn from the rabbi but also imitate the rabbi. The disciples would spend all day, every day following, listening, learning, and copying the rabbi—in essence becoming like the rabbi. I refer the reader to the extensive work and wisdom of Ray Vander Laan for detailed studies on the relationship of the disciple to the rabbi along with many other topics.

Jesus has just chosen and called his disciples. Their training is beginning. These young men need a change in perspective. They need to unlearn a lot of their training in the law. Anyone who has gone through basic training in the military can relate to these men. Jesus needs to help them unlearn some old habits and ways of thought and instill in them a new set of rules and code of conduct.

Jesus calls his disciples together to begin their training. He starts with the Beatitudes. They are the bridge, coming after His call of the disciples and before He explains the spiritual, not physical, implications of the new life being set before them. Jesus is getting ready to give them new insight into the old law. The climax of His dissertation comes in verse 48, where He says, "Therefore you shall be perfect, just as your Father in Heaven is perfect."

The Beatitudes show the growth of Christian discipleship. They are the bridge that ties the theory of the law and the new interruption and application together. Jesus first covers being poor in spirit, mourning (sorrow), meekness (humility), and seeking righteousness (hunger and thirst). These deal with God reaching out to man and our response. Jesus then covers mercy, pure hearts, and being peacemakers. These deal with how we are to respond and interact with the unsaved world around us. Jesus covers persecution and rejection third; these deal with the world's response to us as His disciples. Jesus lastly declares the victory celebration that awaits us as we cross the finish line.

Jesus is up-front about the disciples' past without Him, what it will mean to them to follow Him, and what He promises at the end of the journey. Jesus uses the Beatitudes to show His disciples the path they must follow to change from who they are to who they must become to complete the journey in becoming a disciple, in becoming like their Master.

Nothing has changed! The Beatitudes are a short and concise step-by-step revelation of the journey we all must make to become a true disciple of our Rabbi, our Lord, our Adonai, our Ruler and Master, to become one who wants to be more than a follower, who wants to be like the Master. It takes time, commitment, effort, and sacrifice. A disciple must be willing to lose this life to be transformed into the image of our Master. It is a process without shortcuts.

The road laid out by the Beatitudes reveals the need to gain victory over the internal battle of sin raging in the heart before we can win the external battle over evil in the world. Jesus gives us a clear pathway of character growth and spends the rest of the Sermon on the Mount using easy-to-understand examples to illustrate His points. He does not get overly spiritual; He uses personal experiences to show the need for character growth, the need to change what is residing in the depths of our hearts instead of our heads; the "what we should do" resides in our heads, but the heart controls our actual actions.

I did not start out to write a book on discipleship. My original intent was to write a short Bible study on the Beatitudes. But the Beatitudes are a study in discipleship, a guide for the follower of Jesus to become something more: a disciple.

A follower may believe that Jesus is the Christ. A follower may even repent of his or her sins and accept His atoning work on the cross. A follower may even want to share the Good News of Jesus with others. But being a disciple? That is a different issue altogether!

Disciples do not want just to be followers. Disciples do not want just to serve Jesus. They want much more. Disciples want to get close to Jesus, so close that their lives become identified with Jesus—their rabbi. They want to so identify with, copy, and imitate Jesus that they become like Jesus. Their goal is to become so much like their rabbi that they are willing to lose their lives for His. The goal is that when people look at a disciple, they see the rabbi.

That is our goal. Our goal as a disciple is to become so identified with our rabbi, our Lord and Master, that we reflect Him to the world. Our goals and concerns get absorbed into His Will. We are no longer masters of our own lives. We are His servants and stewards of His Word to the world. We are accountable only to Him for the faithful completion of His purpose in our lives.

We can lose focus and spend a lot of time trying to fight sin in our life, trying either to please God or earn our position in heaven. We must realize we cannot fight sin; we must die to it! When we finally "die" to this life, God, who is faithful, gives us a new life and renewed spirit. We are adopted into the family of God and called His children.

> I have been crucified with Christ; it is no longer
> I who live, but Christ lives in me; and the life
> which I now live in the flesh I live by faith in the
> Son of God, who loved me and gave Himself for
> me (Galatians 2:20).

The disciple has one purpose and one purpose only: to live a life that pleases his or her rabbi at all times (2 Corinthians 5:9).

My purpose is not to engage in a major discourse on each of the character traits found in the Beatitudes. There are many who are more qualified than I am for that discussion. My goal is to introduce a new perspective on some of the most cherished and preached-about verses in the Bible. My goal is to help those believers who have become confused and disoriented in their spiritual lives. My goal is to help those believers who are longing for deeper relationships with God during these most challenging times. It can get confusing.

Why is this step-by-step guide to discipleship being revealed today? Why did our Lord use me and not someone famous? I do not know. I never intended to write a book. All I can say is that God sometimes uses donkeys.

Let us start the journey.

CHAPTER ONE

Blessed are the poor in spirit

Blessed are the poor in spirit, for theirs is the kingdom of God
—Matthew 5:3

Have you ever been poor? I mean living in the streets, not knowing where you would sleep or what you would eat poor? Probably not! Neither have I. But I suspect you may know or have known someone in that condition. A lot of these individuals may not have had much for such a long time that their current condition has become their new normal; they are used to it by now. They are running on empty financially, emotionally, and spiritually. They do not know where to turn for help, so they just keep on going, and one day blends into the next.

There is another segment of poor today, but you do not recognize them as easily. You may live next to one of them; you may even be one of them. These are the ones who look like they have it all—nice home, nice car, nice clothes—and they mingle with all the nice people. But if you looked inside of their lives you might find they have lost their jobs some time ago, banks are ready to foreclose on their homes, and their cars are about to be repossessed. They have maxed out their credit cards, and they are so enslaved to the world around them that they do not know what to do or whom to turn to. Their marriages died a long time ago because they were working too much. Their children do not know them. They are emotionally bankrupt. These are the working poor. They are as financially, emotionally, and spiritually empty as the homeless people on the street.

During the slave trade, prisoners were sometimes placed in spaces no bigger than four feet by eighteen inches. Their feet, hands, and necks were shackled so they could not even move much less escape. I suspect many of the working poor I described above feel the same way. The world promised them money, fame, big homes, important job titles—access to the good life. They found the more they bought into the good life, the more enslaved they became and the less freedom they had, the less control they had over their own lives. In the end they felt as trapped as the prisoners on those slave ships.

Both individuals are trapped and prisoners of their situation. They are enslaved in the world system. Both will stay enslaved unless they change their outlook and focus. They need to stop looking down at their position and start looking up to their Provider. God gives us two examples in the Bible that illustrate this point.

The first example is found in the Book of Job. You might know the story: Job was doing everything right; God had blessed him with money, a large family, friends, and a lot of cattle.

Job found himself in the middle of an object lesson between God and Satan (Job 1:1-12). Job has everything taken away: money, home, health, family, and cattle—all gone. The rest of the book plays out like a courtroom drama. Job finally realizes his position; he is finally running on empty. He gets to the point that he realizes he was spiritually going in the wrong direction and did not even know it. He was lost.

> I have heard of You by the hearing of the ear, But know my eye sees You. Therefore, I abhor myself, And repent in dust and ashes (Job 42:5-6).

The other example is the Prodigal Son (Luke 15:11-32). He was a pampered, spoiled kid who wanted something he had not even merited or earned. He wanted his future inheritance right then; he did not want to honor his father by continuing to work the farm and inherit his share after his father passed away—he wanted it immediately! His father gave it to him, and the son took it and was gone! The world awaited him. The night life was the good life for him—until the money ran out. He ended up on the street, or in this case a pig pen! One must remember that for a Jew this was as low as anyone could get—the end of the line. Where could he go but back to his father? He had to hit bottom to look up.

> I will arise and go to my father, and will say to him, "Father, I have sinned against heaven and you, and I am no longer worthy to be called your son. Make me like one of your hired servants"(Luke 15:18-19).

It is no coincidence that both had to become financially and physically broke to see they were both spiritually broke as well. They both needed to become aware of their real condition. They needed to recognize where they were, repent for their past actions, and return to their father. In New Testament terms they needed to die to their old selves and be reborn into a new relationship, a new perspective, and a new life. They need to turn their backs on the world and focus their attention back to God the Father.

The first step on the road to discipleship is to recognize we are spiritually bankrupt, dead in the water with no way out. We have hit bottom. We need to stop looking within and start looking without, to the Savior.

We must remember this is God's plan. He has prepared the Way. He has thought everything out to make it as clear as possible for us. The biggest hindrance to starting our growth as disciples is being simply too full of ourselves: prideful, arrogant, and envious. In a word—sin. We are fighting battles we cannot win by ourselves. Once we finally realize that the value system of this life is literally killing us, we can start our journey back. We have traveled a road seeking money, power, position, love, peace, joy, and security only to find out we have been going in the wrong direction. We work harder and longer just to find out we are on the wrong road. We keep trying to obey a list of do's and don'ts just to find out the list keeps getting bigger and bigger. Somewhere along the way we wandered away from God. We got lost!

Don't you hate getting lost? I do. I especially dislike getting lost when traveling with my wife. I admit it. It is true. We guys hate to ask for directions. I am going down the freeway, making really good time, and all of a sudden something just doesn't seem right. I am not really sure, but I get this feeling I am not where I want to be. Then I hear those words. You guys know the words: "Honey, are you sure we're going in right direction?" "Yes!" I say this knowing that she is nicely telling me we are not. I just do not want to admit I have made a mistake. For some really crazy reason I believe if I just keep going down the road, the problem will fix itself. So by the time I humble myself and admit she is right, we are several more miles down the road; we have wasted precious time and energy, and we must stop, turn around, and start back. Life is a lot like that.

We find ourselves traveling down this life guided by worldly standards. The longer we are on the road, the more we feel something is just not right. A small voice keeps telling us we are going in the wrong direction, but we do not want to listen. This road seems fun and exciting, just not right! We feel somehow things will work out if we go faster, travel longer, or work harder. But it doesn't work that way. Many, like Job, end up losing everything they are working to secure. We must stop, admit our condition, turn around, and let a new Guide show us the way.

Jesus is our Guide.

> I am the way, the truth, and the life. No one comes to the Father except through Me (John 14:6).

What does God promise us when we admit we are lost? God promises He will dwell with the humble and contrite in heart. He promises a place in His heaven for all those who finally realize that while they were feeding their worldly flesh they were starving their spirits. He also cautions that all those who never get to that point in their lives will never know peace and rest (Isaiah 57:14-21).

When we realize our condition, when we come to the end of the road with nowhere to go, when we are empty and broken, we find the only thing to do is turn back toward the God from Whom we have been running. When we make that turn, when we repent, we find to our surprise He has been near us all the time (Psalms 34:18).

Don't you just hate when people quote old adages? I do! If you are like me, adages and platitudes just make me crazy. The problem is that they are so true. So get ready to go crazy:

When all else fails, read the instructions.

The Bible is God's instruction manual for life given to the world! We just sometimes get off course and try to do things our own way.

Jesus makes this clear when He begins His ministry. He walks right into a synagogue and starts reading out of the book of Isaiah that God the Father has sent Him to share the news of God's plan. He has been sent to heal the broken in heart and to free those who are oppressed (Luke 4:16-20). Jesus sits down after reading the passage, an indication at that time that the Scriptures are completed or fulfilled.

So do we want to start on this journey of discipleship? We must realize our condition. Our spirit is running on empty. We realize we cannot keep doing what we have been doing and expect different results. We are out of gas, pointed in the wrong direction, and there is no help in sight. It is time to get out the map, the instruction manual—the Bible—and start reading.

The first step is to repent. The draw of Satan and the world is great. We must willfully turn our backs to this world, but this is not easy. We have sinned against God and deserve the only sentence for sin—death. But once we make the decision to start the walk back to God with a truly humble spirit, we find that God will lift us up (James 4:7-10).

We need to acknowledge our condition to God and before man that we are sinning against God and turn back to Him. We accept the fact that the only sentence for sin is death. We acknowledge that Christ paid the price for us (Romans 6:23).

We die to this world and the sin in it so He gives us a new life in Christ. We stop fighting sin and die to it.

What will He do? He promises to forgive us our sins and to provide us power in the form of God the Holy Spirit to enable us to take the next step (Acts 2:36-39). Any journey starts with the first step!

I know; you are thinking you need to do something more. You must pay Him back for all the pain you have caused Him. You need some kind of peace offering. You, You, You. Nope! That is not how you get into God's kingdom!

> With what shall I come before the LORD, And bow myself before the High God? Shall I come before Him with burnt offerings, With calves a year old? Will the LORD be pleased with thousands of rams, ten thousand rivers of oil? Shall I give my firstborn for my transgressions, the fruit of my body for the sin of my soul? He has shown you, O man, what is the good: And what does the LORD require of you But to do justly, To Love mercy, And to walk humble with your God?(Micah 6:6-8).

Jesus has already done the rest!

Many believers today have detoured off God's path for their lives. They are trying to live in two worlds: the world of the flesh and the Devil, and God's world. They are trying to serve two masters. They just need to get back on course. Do you want to get back on the straight path to God? Do you want more than what you have? Do you want to start on the road of discipleship? The first step is gaining a poor, humble spirit that is ready to repent and acknowledge your sins to God. You might as well. He already knows. It is not a secret!

> If we confess our sins, He is faithful and just to forgive us our sins and to cleanse us from all unrighteousness (1 John 1:9).

We have really only one real choice in this life: We get to choose which master we will serve!

> And if it seems evil to you to serve the Lord, choose for yourselves this day whom you will serve, whether the gods which your fathers served that were on the other side of the River. Or the gods of the Amorites, in whose land you dwell. But as for me and my house, we will serve the Lord (Joshua 24:15).

THOUGHTS TO PONDER

1. Is your life a string of dead ends? Do you keep trying the same things hoping for different results? Is your Jesus only a part-time Savior? Are you finally at a place where you will admit you cannot help yourself? Lonely? Scared? Tired? Feeling useless? Spiritually bankrupt? Write down your feeling so you will not forget them.

2. Jesus came to pay your debt—all of it. He is ready to redeem, restore, and refresh you. You need to take the first step and confess how you have rebelled against His rules—your sins against God, the secret ones you wanted to keep. Don't worry—He already knows. You just need to admit them to yourself. Write them down.

3. Take a deep breath. It should feel good to get all that stuff out in the open instead of trying to hide it. Smile! You now have a real Guide—His Name is Jesus. You are now on a new journey. What are your feelings about the future?

CHAPTER TWO

Blessed are those who mourn

Blessed are those who mourn, for they shall be comforted.
—MATTHEW 5:4

The first response to our realization we have been going in the wrong direction is to stop, turn around, and start on the straight road back to God. That first step on our return journey brings us face-to-face with the Living God (we just did that in the last chapter). The light of the Lord fills our soul to reveal its true condition. We know we have sinned and need a Savior. We have no idea how bad it is until the light of the Lord fills our hearts and souls. It is like cleaning a room in the dark. We might think it is clean, but when we open the curtains and let the light shine in, that light shows us we have not cleaned anything, we have just been moving the dirt from one area to the other. The first encounter with the Living, Resurrected Lord fills us with remorse and a true sense of sorrow and anguish for our sins. We feel the need to repent for what we have done to Him.

Most of us have never been in prison, but I have known some who have. I am told it is not a nice experience. The beds are not comfortable, the food is terrible, and the company is not always friendly. One time is normally enough for the average person to learn he or she does not want to go back. During the time of Jesus, one was put in prison for debts owed. A list of the debts was posted on the cell door, and the debtor could not get out until the debts were paid. The debtor was in prison, so how were debts to be paid off if someone did not come to help? It must have felt like a hopeless situation.

What a joy it must have been when someone came and paid off the debts. It was finished! The price had been paid. The cell door was opened, and the debtor was free! I suspect there were tears of joy and hugs and kisses going around. Someone in prison was now free. That is what Jesus does for you and me.

> And you, being dead in your transposes and the uncircumcision of your flesh, having forgiven you all trespasses, having wiped out the handwriting of requirements that was against us, which was contrary to us. And He has taken it out of the way, having nailed it to the cross (Colossians 2:14).

We mourn and cry out once we realize we are in a cell, trapped by sin and shame. Jesus is the only One Who can pay the price to set us free. We want nothing more than to get closer to Him. We want to know things have been made right. We want to be clean before our Lord. The revelation of our true condition brings mourning and weeping as we become aware of how far off the mark we had gone (remember the Prodigal Son). It was not just what we did, but what we thought (Hebrews 4:12-13). How long we have traveled in the wrong direction. How much time we have lost with the One Who loves us the most.

> Draw near to God and He will draw neat to you. Cleanse your hands, you sinners: and purify your hearts, you double-minded. Lament and mourn and weep! Let your laughter be turned to mourning and your joy to gloom. Humble yourselves in the sight of the Lord, and He will lift you up (James 4:8-10).

I remember growing up. All I wanted as a little boy was to make my father proud of me. There was nothing better in the world than to get a big smile from Dad for a job well done. The other side of the coin, however, was not as nice. Nothing made me feel like a failure more than getting punished for doing something really naughty. The only thing that made life right again was to tell my Dad I was sorry. It normally ended with me crawling up into his lap and crying as I felt his loving arms wrap around me. I knew my relationship with my father had been restored.

Have you ever really messed up a relationship? All of a sudden you find yourself shying away from that person. Days turn into weeks, and weeks turn into months. In my case the months turned into years. The person in my life was my brother, the one who created the illustrations in this book. I can never recapture the time I lost away from my brother. In the same way we can never recapture the lost time away from our Lord, our Rabbi, the One Whom we are trying to imitate.

Our mourning must come from a true acknowledgment of our condition. It must come from the depth of our soul. It comes out of true sorrow. As with Peter, it is a mourning that comes from knowing we have fallen short of God's purpose for our lives (Matthew 26:69-75). Our sorrow leads to confession and the desire to be cleansed of our sins. Our sorrow makes us want to get "right" with God. We realize we must destroy the "strongholds of sin in our minds" (2 Corinthians 7:11, 10:4-6).

We also recognize that it is not only about us. Once we truly, deep down in our soul realize our condition, we remember those who do not know Christ are trapped in the same prisons of sin and shame. What about our family, our friends, and those around us? What about them?

Jesus cried out and mourned for others. As we start to become more like our Rabbi, we start looking outward to our family, friends, and the world, to all those who exist without the knowledge of Jesus and what He has done for their sin-sick souls. We cry out in anguish and mourn for those who do not know the comfort that can be theirs by allowing Christ to forgive and comfort them.

It would be so much easier if we were in physical prisons. We could see our condition. The problem is that the prison we find ourselves is not something we can see, smell, or touch. It is a spiritual prison that enslaves the unbeliever. The believer realizes the physical can never enslave or imprison the spirit set free by Christ, but the unbeliever does not realize the bars of sin that enslave the spirit.

The saddest part of it all is that those still sitting in prison cells of sin and shame could walk out any time they wanted. Jesus paid their debts at the same time He paid the debts for you and me. The locks on their cell doors are removed, and they are free to leave. The cost to them for their freedom? Acknowledging Jesus, the Christ, as their Benefactor. Jesus—the One Who paid the price they could not pay. They need to acknowledge and confess their condition. They need to accept the payment paid by the Savior.

We mourn and cry for those who refuse to accept Jesus as their Savior. We continue to pray they will eventually see the Light. The example that come to mind is the story of the two men nailed to crosses alongside Jesus (Luke 23:31-32). The one continues to mock Jesus, but the other comes to his senses. "Hey You! We're here because we deserve to be. We're getting just what the law dictates. This guy has done nothing wrong! Jesus, have mercy on me. Maybe You could remember me. Maybe You could find a small place in Your Kingdom for me." (I paraphrase).

> For it pleased the Father that in Him all the fullness should dwell, and by Him to reconcile all things to Himself, by Him, whether things on earth or things in heaven, having made peace through the blood of His cross (Colossians 1:20).

Both prisoners died nailed to crosses. The one died in his sins, alone and separate from God. The other was set free. The nails no longer held him captive. He was reconciled to God; he was not alone. We must take comfort in the knowledge that Jesus is infinite in His Mercy and absolutely just. He is not arbitrary! There will be no surprises. In the end, everyone has a choice.

The blessed are those of us who respond to God's call before it is too late. All mankind will eventually experience the piercing brightness of God's Light on our souls. Some, like Peter, will weep and cling to Christ, while others, like Judas, will attempt to correct their sins themselves. They will finally realize they cannot turn back the clock on righteousness. Their remorse will lead to death, the natural result of sin (Matthew 27:3-5).

What is God's response to our honest acknowledgment of our condition? What does He do when our hearts cry out for more of Him? His response is not one of harshness but of help—think about the prisoner on the cross.

> Therefore you now have sorrow: but I will see you again and your heart will rejoice, and your joy no one will take away from you (John 16:22).

Jesus promises to not leave us alone. He promises to be with us as we proceed on our journey to become like Him. Jesus promises to answer our cries of remorse. He promises to empower us with God the Holy Spirit. He promises He will come back to collect those of us who remain at the end of the Age (John 14:12-16).

Jesus also promises to throw us a party even better than the Prodigal Son's feast. I do not know about you, but the feast at the Marriage Supper of the Lamb sure sounds like a party to me (Revelation 19:7-10).

We are filled with joy, knowing the internal power and guidance of the Holy Spirit will guard and guide us. We will no longer be the slaves of the external laws that only enslave and condemn. We will have an internal guidance system, the Holy Spirit, to keep us on course.

Out of conviction comes confession. Out of confession comes comfort. With comfort from Jesus comes the power to comfort others.

> Therefore comfort each other and edify one another, just as you are doing (1 Thessalonians 5:11).

Keep telling those still sitting in their cells of sin that they are free to go. A disciple will allow the comfort received from above to flow out to others.

We continue to grow vertically to Christ so that we can continue to minister horizontally to the world.

THOUGHTS TO PONDER

1. You are now aware of just how much you have hurt, rebelled against, and totally rejected the One Who loved you enough to die on the cross for you. He died to restore the relationship you worked so hard to destroy. He now wraps you in His arms and wipes away your tears. What emotions are running through you?

2. Your position with God has changed. You are now one of His children. You are now free to follow Him without fear of being thrown out. How does that security as a child of the Living God make you feel?

3. You were a prisoner sentenced to life without parole. Jesus not only set you free, He also expunged your record. It is like the crimes were never committed. He has wiped away your past sins and your tears of sorrow and hurt. You can feel secure with your new life. What will you do with it?

CHAPTER THREE

Blessed are the meek

Blessed are the meek, for they shall inherit the earth.
—Matthew 5:5

The word "meek" conveys humility, gentleness, and controlled self-discipline. Once disciples of Christ truly understand the condition of their souls and receive the gift of the Holy Spirit, they are new creations. Their lives can never be the same. They are aware that their lives are not their own. They walk in a spirit of humility because they know God is in control. They can no longer take credit for anything life brings. Their lives are independent of the events that surround and impact it.

Disciples walk in a spirit of controlled self-disciple because they are lead and guided by the Holy Spirit. We are the "elect of God." We are special.

> Therefore, as the elect of God, holy and beloved, put on tender mercies, kindness, humility, meekness, long suffering (Colossians 3:12).

God is in control of our situation, so the disciple should respond to every trial and temptation as an opportunity to reflect God's Grace and exercise their faith. Just as a bodybuilder uses weights to exercise and strengthen muscles, God uses trials and temptations to help disciples use and strengthen their faith. After all, we are the army of God.

This strength does not depend on us. It comes from the inner strength firmly established on our new relationship with and trust in the Risen Lord (Psalms 37:5-11). We can withstand the evils of the world because we know what awaits us. We know Who is in control. We know the rantings and ravings of this world are of no effect in the end. We need to view this present age through the rearview mirror of the future. We know we are joint heirs with Jesus (Romans 8:16-17). We will inherit the God's Kingdom.

> Then the King will say to those on His right hand, "Come, you blessed of My Father, inherit the kingdom prepared for you from the foundations of the world" (Matthew 25:34).

Let that last thought sink in. God promises believers they will inherit the earth. How do we respond to the events around us when we finally realize they do not really matter? Do we respond like our Rabbi or like the world?

Anyone can give into worldly passions and emotions. Vengeance and hate are easy and normal reactions to the attacks of the world. The news is filled with acts of violence against anything that upsets us: beatings, shootings, road rage, and anything else that hinders us from getting our own way. It takes a gentleness rooted and grounded in self-control to do otherwise, to respond out of love and not out of hurt and hate!

I suppose some of you are naturally gentle, without a mean bone in your body. I confess I cannot relate to you. My experience is that the "natural" person will revert to the innate passions of the worldly spirit unless trained and brought under control by an outside force. Our inner passions must have boundaries or limits that control our actions. These boundaries are laws and rules in the physical world. The boundaries of the spirit are those set by God the Holy Spirit for the disciple.

Anyone in the military during the Vietnam War knows what I mean. We were not treated very well in California where I was stationed. But I represented the Air Force, the military, and my country. We were under orders not to respond in any way to the less-than-kind words and hand gestures shown us during those years. We were trained to obey orders, and our orders were to not react or retaliate. It was not about us. The anger was directed not against us personally but against what we represented. Isn't that the same with a disciple of our Lord, Jesus? The world and its evils do not really hate us. The world hates Who we represent—our Lord.

Some of the most soft-spoken people I know were in some sort of Special Forces unit. Nothing riled them. It was their training. They were trained to objectively respond to their surrounding and not let emotions control their actions. I also think part of it was their inner knowledge that the ranting going on around them was insignificant compared to the strength and power they could bring to the situation. Great power, once released, can have devastating results. Little dogs tend to yap the loudest, while big dogs just need to stare at you.

It takes true power to respond out of love rather than react out of hate as the world would expect. Paul alludes to this while writing his second letter to the Corinthians (2 Corinthians 13:1-4). He is cautioning them not to take his controlled response to their attack on his authority as weakness. He cautions them that just as the world falsely equated Christ's death on the cross as weakness, they should not equate Paul's response to them as weakness. His outward meekness is coupled with the inner authority and power of God in his life.

The disciple has the freedom to respond with love because the disciple is guided and empowered by the Holy Spirit that leads us in all Truth. The disciple is controlled by the Spirit and not the flesh. Disciples have died to the flesh that they may live by the Spirit (Luke 6:27-36). People do not tend to lash out in anger when they know they can respond from a position of strength.

We need to understand we cannot withstand the attacks of this world on our own. If we could, we would immediately be filled with the pride of knowing that we could. It is a classic Catch-22 situation. When we think we overcome one sin, we simply fall victim to another. The only thing we can do is throw up our hands and realize we need help. At that point we are finally in the position to receive, with meekness, God's Word, which is placed in out hearts. We are then able to work out what God has placed inside without sin because we know it is not ourselves in control.

No one said becoming a disciple was easy. We are addicted to the emotions of the flesh. It takes a truly broken heart and spirit to allow Christ to replace our lives with His. We move forward in this journey with a meek and humble spirit by remembering our past. We were dead in our sins and are now made alive by our faith in Him. It is only by God's Grace that we can continue our journey (Ephesians 2:1-9).

> Set your minds on things above, not on things on the earth. For you died, and your life is hidden with Christ in God (Colossians 3:2-3).

We need to remember that Christ came to show us the Way. He does not ask us to do anything He has not already done for us. Christ shows us humility by surrendering to the will of the Father in the Garden of Gethsemane (Matthew 26:39). He shows us controlled self-disciple on the cross (1 Peter 2:18-25).

Our Master tells us He came to "preach the gospel to the poor," to "heal the brokenhearted," to "proclaim liberty to the captives," to give "sight to the blind," and set free "those who are oppressed" (Luke 4:18-19). He tells us to do it because He did it.

> Then He called His twelve disciples together and gave them power and authority over all demons, and diseases. He sent them to preach the kingdom of God and heal the sick (Luke 9:1-2).

What drives us to follow our Rabbi? We were once poor in spirit. We were once rebellious against God. We were once prisoners of sin. We were once blind but now see. We were once oppressed. We follow Jesus in a state of meekness and humility because we know our sinful past. We understand and regret our rebellion against God. We know and experience His Mercy daily as we live for Him. We live a life in response to what God has already done through Jesus. We do it because we have been set free and want to tell somebody, anybody, about the freedom we have through faith in Jesus.

The objective of disciples is to become like their Rabbi. We can take up the yoke of our Rabbi through the power of the Helper, the Holy Spirit, that Christ leaves us (Matthew 11:29-30).

Our spirit is made free (Romans 8:1-2).

Our spirit is given peaceful assurance (John 16:33).

Our spirit is strengthened and empowered (Acts 1:8).

We are no longer sustained by the world but by the Word (John 6:51).

> The Spirit Himself bears witness with our spirit that we are children of God, and if children, then heirs—heirs of God and joint heirs with Christ, if indeed we suffer with Him, that we may also be glorified together (Romans 8:16-17).

We can rejoice and be glad. We get it all!

THOUGHTS TO PONDER

1. What parts of your life do you still need to give over to God? These are the parts that will take constant surrender and communication with God.

2. What actions can you take to reduce the worldly passions and emotions in your life?

3. What steps can you take today to bring your life and thoughts more in line with the mind of Christ?

Blessed are those who hunger and thirst

Blessed are those who hunger and thirst for
righteousness for they shall be filled.
—MATTHEW 5:6

What makes people hunger and thirst for something? What causes such a craving that they seek more of it at all cost? One reason could be because they have been deprived of it for so long that their bodies are crying out for it just to survive. The other reason could just be that they found something so wonderful, something so satisfying that they cannot seem to get enough of it. I am not talking about a sinful addiction such as narcotics; I am talking about a fantastic pizza or a great bowl of ice cream on a hot day (you now know my weaknesses). What do you crave? We should all crave the righteousness of God.

> For the Lord is righteous, He loves righteousness:
> His countenance beholds the upright (Psalms
> 11:7).

Righteousness is sometimes explained as "right standing" with God. That is what happens when we get a taste of our new life with Jesus. We find we have regained our right standing with God through Jesus. We realize we never want to lose our right standing, our righteousness, again.

What are we really craving? We crave more of Jesus. We seek Him at all costs. All costs! That even means being totally committed and submitted to God. The unsaved keep trying to do it themselves, but the disciple is aware that righteousness comes only through Jesus, the Christ. Paul explains it this way:

> For they being ignorant of God's righteousness,
> and seeking to establish their own righteousness,
> have not submitted to the righteousness of God.
> For Christ is the end of the law for righteousness
> to everyone who believes (Romans 10:3-4).

I remember when my wife and I were newly married; we once went on a hike in a state park on a hot summer day. We made two big mistakes: we failed to realize how long it would take us to complete the trail, and we failed to prepare for the lack of water fountains that generally accompany such trails in other state parks. The result was that after completing the trail a couple of hours later we were thirsty. I mean ready-to-collapse, give-me-some-water-now thirsty. Our bodies knew what was missing, and they needed water immediately. When we found some, we drank and drank and drank. We did not want to leave the fountain.

The same thing must happen to travelers in a desert. When they come to an oasis, they may be so thirsty that they smell the water. If it is not readily available, they will dig for it. They will do anything to get it because their lives depend on it. The disciple of our Lord Jesus is in the same position. Paul says in his sermon to the leaders in Greece that we are to grope after God.

> So that they should seek the Lord, in the hope
> that they might grope for Him and find Him,
> though He is not far from each one of us (Acts
> 17:27).

What a vivid picture! Disciples should be so hungry for a closer relationship with Christ that they become almost frantic. It is one thing to hunger and thirst for something, but it is another to grope for it. I picture someone reaching, clawing, and tearing away anything and everything to get what he or she needs. Nothing is allowed to get in the way! The world around fades away, and he or she sees only the object of desire. That is the passion and focus being described in this passage. The disciple should be so consumed with getting closer to Christ and His righteousness that nothing will get in the way. Nothing!

Disciples seeking this closer walk with their Rabbi, Jesus, his Lord, will not be burdened with any unneeded baggage. They will discard anything that hinders their getting closer. Disciples want to lighten their loads as they run the race toward Christ and His Righteousness without any thought of pain or discomfort (Hebrews 12:1-3).

There is an interesting corollary to this idea. The closer we get to one thing, the farther we must naturally be getting from another. The more time disciples spend getting closer to Jesus, the less time they spend in the world and the farther away they get from it. They spend less time thinking about the world, and they find themselves spending less time needing or even wanting it. Disciples are slowly weaned off the physical, emotional, and spiritual desires of the world as the Holy Spirit fills their souls.

Jesus is the Bread of Life. He is the Living Water. He provides the only Source of Life that will truly fill us. Communion is one of the most beautiful and vivid practices of the church. It is a regular reminder that our spiritual life is fed and sustained by the body and blood of our dear Lord and Savior. It is a reminder that without the shedding of blood there is no remission of sin. Righteousness can come only through Christ (Hebrews 9:22).

> Whoever drinks of this water will thirst again, but whoever drinks of the water I shall give him will never thirst. But the water that I shall give him will become in him a fountain of water springing up into everlasting life. I am the Bread of Life (John 4:13-14, 6:48).

Disciples of Christ, once filled with the Holy Spirit and rescued from the bondage of their fleshly emotions and sinful past, start to drink from the fountain of Living Water. They realize their spirits have been deprived of the real Water they need to survive, grow, and flourish. The spirit wants to drink in the only Water that can provide the righteousness it needs to live the life it was meant to live. Physical water can satisfy the flesh, but only the Living Water of Christ can satisfy the spirit.

The disciple continuously seeks after Christ and His Living Water. The disciple understands the spirit needs to be continuously filled and renewed from the Fountain of Life just as the physical body continuously needs physical water. Jesus is shifting our focus from the world to Himself, and we need this change in perspective because of our mission.

> But seek first the kingdom of God and His righteousness, and all these things shall be added to you (Matthew 6:33).

A disciple has the task of sharing God's Word with the world, of being a witness of God's Love to the lost. A disciple can give out only what come in. Jesus condemns the leaders of His time for trying to do otherwise.

> You have neither heard His voice at any time, nor seen His form. But you do not have His word abiding in you, because whom He sent, Him you do not believe. You search the Scriptures, for in them you think you have eternal life; and these are they which testify of Me (John 5:37-39).

Anyone can search the Scriptures, anyone can gather facts about God (Satan knows much more than we do about God), but a disciple does not seek facts but a relationship!

We are called as disciples to pour out God's Love to the world. We cannot continue to pour out His Love unless we continue to be filled by His Presence. We continue to drink in God's Righteousness so our lives may be poured out to those around us. You have heard it said that "out of the heart, the mouth speaks." Paul says it better:

> That if you confess with your mouth the Lord Jesus and believe in your heart that God has raised Him from the dead, you will be saved. For with the heart one believes into righteousness, and with the mouth confession is made unto salvation (Romans 10:9-10).

Some people have a real problem in this area; they are unwilling to give up their present situations, which they know are not the best, for what they know will be better. This is exactly what happened to many who heard Jesus. They believed everything He was saying—everything! The problem was that to act on that belief would cost them everything they cherished. They were not hungry enough. They would need to totally submit themselves to Him, but they were just too busy doing what seemed comfortable and easy to them. It just did not seem like the right time.

Many years ago, C. S. Lewis wrote The Screwtape Letters. In the book, a senior devil is helping his nephew capture his first soul for Satan. The nephew is frustrated because the human kept bringing up Jesus and the need to believe in Him. The uncle provided the answer. Agree with everything the human says. Just tell him he does not need to do it today. Have fun today. You can always accept Jesus tomorrow—always tomorrow. The problem is that we do not always have tomorrow! We have only today!

Many say the stock market operates on two emotions: fear and greed. It would not be much of a stretch to generalize and say that much of the world operates on these same two emotions. This can certainly be said of the people to whom Jesus spoke. To follow Jesus would get them cast out of the synagogue (John 12:37-43). To believe in Jesus is still like that today in many parts of the world. Many of us can simply go to another church if we find ourselves not welcomed where we are at the moment. In the time of Jesus, as today for many people, being cast out of the synagogue (or another place of worship) would mean being cut off from family, friends, and even jobs. No one would hire you or buy your wares. Your family would disown you, your business would dry up, and your position in the community would be destroyed. Believers in America have little knowledge of the sacrifice our fellow Believers are making in other parts of the world.

The disciple must become single-minded in the pursuit of God (Psalms 73:25-26). The spirit starts to control our actions and not the passions and desires of our fleshly body. We become disciplined and focused on becoming like our Rabbi. Nothing else will satisfy our thirst. We have tasted the pure joy and presence of the Lord and want more and more. This continual pursuit finally becomes a lifestyle. It is a lifetime pursuit traveled one step at a time!

> Therefore, laying aside all malice, all deceit, hypocrisy, envy, and all evil speaking, as newborn babes, desire the pure milk of the word, that you may grow thereby, if indeed you have tasted that the Lord is gracious (1 Peter 2:1-3).

This is not easy! It is a perpetual battle between the spirit and the flesh. The flesh would like to simply remodel; God tears down and rebuilds! We must submit to His process and purpose for our lives. We must remember we are strengthened by the Holy Spirit within us.

> . . . do not be conformed to this world, be transformed by the renewing of your mind, that you may prove what is the good and acceptable and prefect will of God (Romans 11:2).

To this day I make certain we never go on a trip without water. I remember how we felt when we did not have it for a time, how much we craved it, and how much trouble we found ourselves in by not being prepared. We must prepare our souls each day in the same way. We need to remember the condition of our souls without the filling of the Living Water. The people of Israel were allowed to wander in the desert for forty years so they would realize their condition. Each of us was allowed to wander in our own desert before finding the Living Water (Deuteronomy 8:1-3). God finally answered the cries of the nation of Israel just as Jesus answers our cries today. We have been in the desert too long. We cry out, and Jesus answers. Come to me. Jesus will give you Living Water.

> On the last day, that great day of the feast, Jesus stood and cried out, saying, If anyone thirsts, let him come to Me and drink. He who believes in Me, as the Scripture has said, out of his heart will flow rivers of living water (John 7:37-38).

Do you hear your Rabbi? Drink! Drink! Drink and fill your spirit, for out of the disciple's heart will flow the Living Water. You need it! The thirsty spirits around you need it!

THOUGHTS TO PONDER

1. What tools, habits, or behaviors were you using in an attempt to fill the gaps in your life before you committed your life to Christ?

2. What feelings and emotions are now so intense that you simply want more and more?

3. What will it cost you to satisfy the thirst and hunger you now feel? What will it cost you to get more and more of the Living Water Jesus provides your soul? Are you ready to pay that price?

CHAPTER FIVE

Blessed are the merciful

Blessed are the merciful, for they shall obtain mercy.
—Matthew 5:7

I remember when we lived in base housing when stationed overseas with the Air Force. For those of you not familiar with overseas housing, they are not normally the largest accommodations in the world. We had two small, very active boys who loved to do all those things little boys do. In my travels, I had the opportunity to collect some beautiful porcelain figurines. They were not cheap at the time. I had bought them over time as gifts for my wife for being gone so much. Unfortunately there was no way to safely display them in our small apartment.

I had told my oldest son over and over not to throw things in the house. Well, you know what happened. The boys were playing and managed to knock over one of the best figurines. I was furious! I sent him to his room to await his doom. I was prepared to really lay out some well-deserved (in my mind at least) judgment. What did he deserve? A spanking? A belt over the bottom? Maybe tar and feathers? The figurine was costly, and the house rule about not throwing things was very clear and well understood (remember we are talking about a five-year-old). The infraction was premeditated and willful. There was only one course of action for such a grievous violation of my very clear orders. I went into his room after letting him wait for the judgment he knew was due him. I explained that the punishment for such willful disobedience. I then forgave him. Why? Because that is what Christ did for me. We both hugged and cried together. Make no mistake. My son knew what he deserved. I, also, know exactly what I deserve.

I am not implying in any way that my thought process was rational, but I hope you get the point. God loves us. He is very clear in telling us His rules and the consequences, but we willfully disobey. Actually, we are no more capable of following His rules than my five-year-old was capable of following my rules.

What is the proper punishment for our disobedience of God's commands? The only answer possible is eternal banishment to hell. Someone needs to pay for our disobedience. God would not be just otherwise. But God loves us, so He can either punish the entire human race or forgive us through His infinite Mercy. He chooses to show mercy.

> For I will be merciful to their unrighteousness,
> and their sins and their lawless deeds I will
> remember no more (Hebrews 8:10).

We forgive because we are first forgiven. Mercy is the active ingredient in our lives that reaches out to bring hope and comfort to the spirit suffering from the pain of sin. It is not a passive desire of the heart; it is the "boots on the ground" and get-dirty part of interacting with the lost and hurting world.

A woman was brought before Jesus for committing adultery. The men wanted to test Jesus—you know the story. Jesus started to write in the dirt. As he wrote, the men slipped away, leaving only the woman to face Jesus (John 8:3-10). We do not really know what He wrote, but we do know what he said to the men.

> He who is without sin among you, let him throw
> the stone at her first (John 8:7).

If we are being honest, we must admit we are no better than the men standing before Jesus. We are quick to condemn others who fall short of our expectations. We tend to be quick to be judge, jury, and executioner of others until we realize we are passing judgment on ourselves. We have a change of heart once our spirit is broken; we are filled with remorse and sorrow for our past sins, and we hunger and thirst for a closer relationship with our Master, Savior, and Rabbi, Jesus.

We show mercy to others because we receive mercy ourselves. Notice that we do not show mercy to receive mercy. We show mercy because we know its value. We know how it feels to receive it. We know it is something that is only given, not taken or earned.

Mercy does not come naturally, nor does it come cheap. Hatred and revenge seem to be emotions far more easily aroused in the natural man. An eye for an eye—right! It then makes sense that mercy cannot be expected of a disciple until that disciple's spirit is first filled with the righteousness, love, and mercy that come from the indwelling of Jesus, the Christ.

One aspect of mercy is the ability to show compassion or forgiveness to someone who fails to do what we expect, an act of omission. The other aspect of mercy is the ability to show compassion or forgiveness to someone who has done you wrong and deserves to be punished (according to your standards), an act of commission. The first is simply the withholding of the power to punish. The second is the expunging of righteous judgment from one who is fully aware of what he or she deserves. We tend to focus on the latter; God is concerned about both.

Disciples of Christ, once aware of the mercy shown for their past sins and filled with the righteousness of the Lord, cannot help but show that same mercy to others. The disciple of Christ is becoming the image of the Master. The Lord shows us by His example what He requires of us. External sacrifices will no longer suffice. The Eternal and Risen Lord wants nothing less than our hearts and souls.

> He has shown you, O man, what is good: And what does the Lord require of you but to do justly, to love mercy, and to walk humbly with your God? (Micah 6:8).

Please notice that God does not want us to simply do it as part of the job. He wants us to love mercy. That can come only when we fully embrace our relationship with Christ. It takes an internal change by faith to allow the external change in action.

This is a difficult concept for many people. I remember taking the bus downtown while going to school in the 70s. It provided for some great conversations. One day I was talking to a young student from Japan who was here to learn English. She knew I was in the military at the time and wanted to know what I thought of Japan. I told her I considered Japan a friend and ally. She asked about Pearl Harbor. I answered that it was a long time ago and that most Americans had forgiven Japan.

Her answered shocked me! She said, "It must be your Christian faith that allowes you to forgive." She then said something that really shocked me: "We will never forget." The shame for their action still burned in their hearts. Many of them could not forgive themselves even though many Americans had.

We cannot move forward with God if we are still trapped by our past sins. God forgives us through His infinite Grace and Mercy. We must accept His Mercy so we can forgive ourselves and start showing that same mercy and forgiveness to others.

God so loved the world that He sent His only Son (John 3:1). We too must love the world as we become the image of our Rabbi. We, His disciples, are here to put God's Love and Mercy into action. We are His active, tangible, and physical agents of His Compassion and Mercy in the world. We must not just show mercy—we must love to show God's Mercy. Why? We must love mercy because that is what God did for us. We must give what we have already received.

> But love your enemies, do good, and lend, hoping for nothing in return; and your reward will be great, and you will be sons of the Most High. For He is kind to the unthankful and evil. Therefore be merciful, just as your Father is merciful (Luke 6:35-36).

Does it sound like I am talking in circles? Maybe. Think of it as a circular staircase to God. He gives, we give, and He gives back. With each round we are climbing up the staircase. We are getting closer to God. We are getting closer and closer to our Rabbi, the Source of Life and Love. We are becoming more like Him. We are becoming disciples.

THOUGHTS TO PONDER

1. We have all been punished for doing something wrong. What are some of the worst things for which you have been punished? Did you really get what you deserved? Be honest.

2. We have also experienced mercy and forgiveness for some wrongdoing. When did you receive forgiveness? How did you feel?

3. The longer we spend with Christ, the more we start becoming like Him. We realize our sins and how much He has forgiven us. What hurts and hatred can you now release to God?

Blessed are the pure in heart

Blessed are the pure in heart, for they shall see God.
—MATTHEW 5:8

Wow! Now that is a promise! You may ask, How do I get a pure heart? How do I maintain a pure heart once I do get one? What does that even mean? Certainly not holding onto the dirt and filth of the flesh.

Notice that Jesus does not say "clean." He does not say 95 percent pure. He says pure, 100 percent, sin-free pure. There are no gray areas with God. We are not taking about "getting right" with God. We are talking about maintaining our relationship with God. We are talking about "staying right" with God. The pure go to heaven. The impure do not!

> To the pure all things are pure, but to those who are defiled and unbelieving nothing is pure, but even their mind and conscience are defiled (Titus 1:15).

This is a pass-or-fail situation. Pure heart? One hundred percent, and you pass. Impure heart? Zero percent, and you fail. God does not grade on a curve. Sometimes I would like it if He did. I know something about grading on a curve. I wanted to be a math teacher. When I was going to college, I needed to have two upper-division English classes. I did not look forward to any English class let alone an upper-division one. It is my experience that math, science, or geeky types do not really fit in well with English, artsy, or music types. It may be one of those right-brain left-brain things, but it just seems to true. Nevertheless I needed to have two classes, and I decided to take them in summer school. It was normally the practice that summer school was taught by junior college teachers, and the classes tended to be a bit easier.

It met my expectations! The teacher in the English composition class made it easy: we wrote one composition a week. We needed to hand in a minimum of three, and he would average the grades. We could quit when we were happy with the grade. Such a deal! I really needed only a B in the class. The first week I received an A (I was working too hard). The next week I received a B (just the right amount of effort, but I had some cushion). In the third week I received a C (just right, and I was history). Now I know you "purists" are waggling your fingers at me (but we just finished talking about mercy). The issue is that I had my own idea of what I needed to attain my goal. In this case it was just to get through these upper-division English classes with decent grades and get on with becoming a math teacher. That does not work with God. Anything that contaminates the heart makes it impure. My standard does not mean a thing.

What contaminates the heart? All those things that drive us to attain worldly goals and desires: envy, pride, ego, and lust for what we want and do not have. As we discussed earlier, our eyes are slowly redirected to God when we hunger and thirst after righteousness. We seek to focus our lives away from the earthly and to the eternal. We become less and less concerned with the physical and visible things of our life and this earth and more concerned with the invisible and spiritual things of God.

We can start cleaning up the filthy recesses of our heart only by first being filled with the righteousness of God. We are starting to get a clearer picture of how the Beatitudes lay out the step-by-step process of our transformation into the image of our Rabbi. With each step we must be willing give up more of ourselves so the Light of Christ can come in and clean us from the inside out. Paul describes this as the "washing of regeneration and renewing of the Holy Spirit" (Titus 3:5).

I had the great pleasure of going through basic training twice. I say that with more than a tad of sarcasm. The first time was the enlisted basic training program during the Vietnam era. I was young, and it was short and fast. The next time was in Officer Training School several years later. It was twelve weeks long, and I was older and wiser, but the training was more deliberate and calculated.

The highlights of the twelve weeks were the weekends when we could get some reprieve from the training, but to get that reprieve we had to prepare Friday night for the Saturday-morning white-glove inspection. Too many demerits? No liberty. So Friday night we cleaned. I mean we cleaned! Nobody who has not gone through a military white-glove inspection in basic training can truly appreciate what I am saying when I say we cleaned! No piece of dust, no piece of lint, no smudge was allowed anywhere in the barracks. The brightest lights were shined on the darkest corners, and nothing went unnoticed. The barracks had to be perfect—at least on the surface.

When God says we must have a pure heart, He means pure. Unfortunately, many people still think the Christian life is like life in the barracks. We will be okay if we just keep the outside looking good. Clean this area, polish that area, put some perfume over here, and everything will be fine. But that does nothing for the inside! Jesus and the disciples kept the ritual of external cleansing before Passover (John 11:55) to fulfill the law (Exodus 23:14-17). But after Passover, a new covenant was given, one that required an internal change of the heart.

The disciple must continuously allow God the Holy Spirit to search and weed out the dark corners of his or her heart. This process of purification is vital because, as we will see later, the disciple is the messenger of God's Light to the world. Any impurity or sin will disrupt, deflect, and diminish that Light.

We take light for granted. It is really a bunch of electrons (forgive me, all you physicists out there). The normal light bulb or flashlight will give out a broad beam that lights up a room. Have you ever noticed what happens when a single ray of sunlight enters a room? All of a sudden you can see the individual pieces of dirt or lint lingering in the air. You did not notice them before because the beam was too broad. You need a really clean room once the light beam gets really small, because a really small light beam will actually be deflected by a piece of lint. Trying to share God's Light and Love out of an impure heart is like trying to shoot an arrow through a tree trunk!

One of my favorite psalms is Psalm 24. It talks about who can stand in God's Holy Place. Only those with clean hands and a pure heart will receive God's blessings and righteousness.

> The earth is the Lord's, and all its fullness, the world and those who dwell therein. For He has founded it upon the seas, and established it upon the waters. Who may ascend into the hill of the Lord? Or who may stand in His holy place? He who has clean hands and a pure heart, Who has not lifted up his soul to an idol, nor sworn deceitfully. He shall receive blessing from the Lord, and righteousness from the God of his salvation (Psalms 24:1-5).

It is not our external actions that get us to heaven; we cannot "work" our way to heaven with anything but actions motivated by a pure heart. God does not care what we do until we are doing it with a pure heart inspected and cleansed by the Light of Christ that penetrates, reveals, and cleanses the sinful recesses of the heart.

This process of discipleship works a bit like an aquifer. Water traveling through the ground is dirty, not drinkable. An aquifer is a natural filter that takes the impurities out of water and leaves it fresh, clear, and crisp. When you taste water straight from an aquifer, all other water tastes terrible. Disciples allow the cleansing power of the Holy Spirit to take the "dirt" from their hearts, leaving them clean before God.

Another example is to compare this process to our liver (forgive me, doctors). Its basic function is to cleanse the body of all the poisons we put into it. When the liver breaks down, the poisons enter the body, and all sorts of not-nice things happen. When we allow "dirt" into our spirit, it poisons it, allowing sin to ooze out into our lives, and not-nice things happen!

The process of discipleship is a filtering process that cleanses us of our sins so we can have pure hearts for God.

Obtaining this "heart transplant" from God is vital to our continued journey in discipleship. It is important because we are being given the stewardship over the mysteries of God. These mysteries are the Grace and Love of God the Father and the salvation that comes only through God the Son, Christ Jesus.

> Let a man so consider us, as servants of Christ and stewards of the mysteries of God. Moreover it is required in stewards that one be found faithful (1 Corinthians 4:1-2).

This stewardship means that we, as His disciples, are responsible for faithfully communicating His message to the world. We are not responsible for its contents or for the results! We are responsible only for sharing God's message with others. Our service to the world is possible only as we are serving God out of pure hearts and pure motives.

Would you serve a meal to a guest on a dirty dish? Would you like to go into surgery where the doctor used dirty instruments? Do like going into a dirty hotel room? How can you expect to put forth the pure word of God from a dirty heart? We are to be clean, a "vessel of honor" prepared to do God's work (2 Timothy 2:21).

A disciple knows the power of showing mercy because a disciple has experienced the Mercy of God. A disciple is able to share a clearer message of the Rabbi as his or her heart becomes cleansed of the filth of the world. It is sometimes referred to as the law of reciprocity.

> Judge not, and you shall not be judged. Condemn not, and you shall not be condemned. Forgive, and you will be forgiven. Give, and it will be given to you: good measure, pressed down,

> shaken together, and running over will be put
> into your bosom. For with the same measure
> that you use, it will be measured back to you
> (Luke 6:37-38).

We show mercy because we get mercy. We share the pure word of God out of a pure heart given us by God. He gives us a pure heart because Jesus, our Rabbi, our Savior, redeemed us (bought us by His blood) from every sinful action (Titus 2:14).

It also means that we are answerable only to Him. This sacred trust and responsibility can be dispensed to the world only with a pure heart. Without it, the message will be contaminated with self-pride, ego, and power that will corrupt. Any sin that accompanies the message will leaven the messenger and the message. The impurities will rise up and corrupt the believer and negate the truth of Christ's sacrificial death on the cross (1 Corinthians 5:1-8).

Disciples with pure hearts are single-focused and not distracted. Nothing can take disciples off the task or journey set before them. Luke explains it is like having two masters.

> No servant can serve two masters; for either he
> will hate the one and love the other, or else he
> will be loyal to one and despise the other. You
> cannot serve God and mammon (Luke 16:13).

A disciple with two masters is like someone with two lovers. No matter how hard a person tries, there is no way to give both lovers undivided attention. Many try, but it always ends in disaster. The disciple cannot have a heart divided between God and the world. We must choose God. After all, this world is passing away (1 John 2:15-17).

Distractions can get us looking in one direction and totally missing something else. One of the greatest recent examples, and a dichotomy in my mind, occurred the first week of September in 1997. The world was in a media frenzy over the death and burial of Princess Diane. The world was subjected to around-the-clock coverage and commentary surrounding this tragic event. But something else happened that week, and the world hardly blinked.

Mother Teresa passed away. She had spent forty-five years feeding the poor. She had been honored with the Nobel Peace Prize in 1979. Her efforts had resulted in 610 missions at the time of her death, but the world hardly noticed her passing!

Both women were famous; both had affected the world around them. Their deaths had significant impact on millions of people. However, the world's reactions to their deaths were dramatically different. With the deepest respect to both women, I submit that one was overcome by the world, and the other overcame the world!

Do you want to have an example of a pure heart? Look to a small, humble, physically worn-out figure who fed the poor for forty-five years.

Jesus explained this idea by referring to a tree bearing fruit (Matthew 12:33-37). You cannot expect a bad tree to bear good fruit. A disciple cannot expect a pure message to come out of a corrupt heart.

> For out of the abundance of the heart the mouth speaks (Matthew 12:34).

We can deceive ourselves into thinking we have pure hearts. It is rather easy if we stay in our prayer closets or just associate with the other "children of God" who go to our church and believe just as we do. Instead of reaching out, we retreat within. It is easy, until you are around little children!

If you want to find out what is inside of you, spend time around little children. They are pure and innocent. They also repeat every word that comes out of your mouth!

> But those things which proceed out of the mouth come from the heart, and they defile a man. For out of the heart proceed evil thoughts, murders, adulteries, fornications, thefts, false witness, blasphemies. These are the things which defile a man (Matthew 15:18-20).

We have three of the most wonderful grandchildren God ever gave grandparents. They love us, and they also let us know every time a "bad" word comes out of our mouths. My wife is not the culprit. I, however, have relapses to my military days from time to time! Yes, I am not perfect; I continue to be a work in progress.

A day with a three-year-old is a true litmus test of the heart. If you do not know one, rent one—it is a great exercise in humility!

Each of us must continually go to the Lord and let the light of His Grace reveal our true selves to us so we can repent and be cleansed. Each disciple has made a decision to become more like his or her Master. Now is the time to get serious. Now is the time to get focused on the task at hand—no holding back, no trying to hide part of our favorite, sinful life. God calls us to be holy, just as He is holy. We must open up our hearts all the way and let the Light of Christ cleanse us and the Holy Spirit fill us so we can love with the pure heart of Christ (1 Peter 1:13-23).

Remember Mother Teresa. The smallest things can have enormous consequences when done out of a pure heart.

We just need to give God our best—He will do the rest!

Can we open our hearts? The next steps are impossible without it!

CHAPTER SIX

THOUGHTS TO PONDER

1. You cannot gauge the condition of your heart. I urge you to get away to someplace where you can be alone. Just ask God to search your heart and reveal the dirt that needs removal, and then be quiet. What did He bring to light? Confess it, and let Him remove it.

2. Do you feel closer to God? You should start seeing Him and hearing Him more clearly. What is He showing you about the journey ahead?

3. You should be starting to look at the world differently. Do you see things in a different light? How have your perceptions been changing?

Blessed are the peacemakers

Blessed are the peacemakers,
For they will be called the sons of God.
—MATTHEW 5:9

Disciples are to become peacemakers. It may be easier to grasp the concept if we say "makers of peace." This is a shift in our focus. We started out concentrating on our relationship with God. Jesus leads us through the need to recognize our sins against God, our repentance of those sins, and our restored relationship with God. Jesus leads us through our renewed desire to get closer to Him and to restore our relationships with others through the mercy He has shown us. Now Jesus is calling His disciples to impact the world around them.

A maker of peace. What a concept! I am writing this during the Christmas season, a time when most in the United States and many around the world celebrate the most wonderful gift given to man by God: the Savior Child, Jesus, God the Son. It is also a time of unprecedented turmoil and unrest. Nations are falling apart, and governments seem totally unprepared and ill-equipped to handle the internal unrest. It is a dichotomy of unequal proportions.

How can we hope to be peacemakers in such a time? We must certainly first work on having peace within ourselves before we can radiate God's Peace to others. How is this possible in today's environment? We need to be honest and admit it is getting increasingly difficult to be at peace with this world and the people in it. The truth is we cannot do it by our own power, which is why we need to be changed. This is the focus of the journey we are on in becoming disciples. Jesus would certainly not expect us to do something without providing us the means to do it.

When the birth of Jesus was announced by the angels in heaven, they declared that peace had come to earth.

> Glory to God in the highest, And on earth peace, goodwill towards men! (Luke 2:14).

The angels were declaring that God's Peace had been given to earth. What did they mean? They certainly did not mean the world would stop experiencing wars. They certainly did not mean mankind would stop fighting amongst themselves. I submit that they were declaring that God's Peace, in the form of the Prince of Peace, had been given to the world that wonderful night in the small town of Bethlehem. This Peace from God was given to man that night and finished years later on cross (Colossians 1:19-20).

Jesus confirms this gift of HIs Peace to the disciples, but the disciples are afraid about what will happen when Jesus is no longer with them.

> Peace I leave with you, My peace I give to you; not as the world gives do I give to you. Let not your heart he troubled, neither let if be afraid. These things I have spoken to you, that in Me you may have peace. In the world you will have tribulation: but be of good cheer, I have overcome the world (John 14:27-33).

The disciple can be a peacemaker only after taking the previous steps in this journey. Notice that all previous steps involve a degree of internal change, a redirection of our lives, and a refocusing on Christ. A disciple must experience spiritual growth through faith in Christ that leads to an active and outward growth to the world. The outward growth is reflected in sharing God's Word with others with the intent of bringing God's Peace to the internal battle over sin raging within them. We are to help them understand the battle is over. We must become more than who we were. We cannot see God with His Peace residing in us (Hebrews 12:14).

> Therefore, if anyone is in Christ, he is a new creation, old things have passed away: behold, all things have become new. Now all things are of God, who has reconciled us to Himself through Jesus Christ, and has given us the ministry of reconciliation, that is, that God was in Christ reconciling the world to Himself, not imputing their trespasses to them, and has committed to us the word of reconciliation (2 Corinthians 5:17-19).

What do I mean about telling them the battle is over? Okay! I mean it is our job to tell them they are continuing to fight a war that is over. They can stop! It is finished! Kaput! Do you know anyone who continued to fight a battle that was already over? I do.

Corporal Shoichi Yokoi fought for Japan in World War II. On the island of Guam, he saw the enemy and hid out in caves until he surrendered in 1972 after being found by some fishermen. He had read leaflets about the war being over, but he did not believe them. He watched people, and he saw planes overhead, but he did not believe it. He needed to have someone tell him that the war was over and that he could go home. He did go home. He died in 1977.

That is what I mean about bringing God's Peace to the world. Many need to hear the message of God's Grace in person. The war is over. The victory is ours!

I must admit this is hard for me. Up to this point it has been mostly about God and me. I have repented of my sins. I mourn over lost relationships and opportunities to have served God. I try to diligently seek after Him. I ask God to cleanse me, use me, and give me a heart transplant. But now He wants me to reach out to others to offer them the same Peace He has given me, people who may not want to hear this Good News and also people who I may not even want to hear the Good News (you can tell God is still working in me as well).

I tend to be a ready, shoot, aim type of guy. I am more than ready to solve a problem, but in the process I become part of the problem. Maybe some of you can relate? Those of us with this internal challenge (no one seems to have problems today) continue to let the Peace of Christ fill us and change us so that we can show that Peace to others.

This is not easy to accept. Things do not always work out the way we want when we try to share the Peace of Christ with the unsaved world. Where does that leave us when we are offended in the process? In what position do we find ourselves when we just want to share the liberating life given us by our relationship with the Risen Lord or when we want to respond in righteous indignation when we are wronged? Can we not strike back when we are wronged? I remind us that we are becoming "righteous," which is different than needing to be proven "right."

Why can't we respond? It is our right, after all! We have earned it, you might say. What about that "eye for an eye" stuff? You may be correct in this world, but God is not of this world, and neither are we! You must also remember that we did not earn anything. You and I are merely recipients of God's Peace, and we are tasked with sharing the Peace of God with others. We are to share how sinful man can be reconciled to the Pure, Perfect, and Most Holy God!

God's plan for His disciples is to be in this world but not of this world. A baby is human from birth and spends the rest of life developing the full potential of being human. The believer born into the family of God, and therefore a child of God, spends the rest of this life becoming more of a child of God. We continue to grow into the persons God wants us to be to fulfill the purpose He intends for us and through us.

As disciples of Christ, we must do all we can to be at peace with those around us because it affects our ability to get close to God. We are told to not even try to come into the presence of God if we are not at peace with others (Matthew 5:22-25).

It is clear that the peace being talked about is not worldly peace; that peace will come only with Christ's return. The peace being talked about in this case is that which is brought to a warring spirit. The Scriptures are talking about the war that rages in the hearts and minds of all people between what they know they should do and what they want to do. We must work to be at peace in our spirit whether or not we can actually make physical peace with those around us.

We know that everyone has the knowledge of God within them (their spirit) but that not everyone responds to that knowledge. Satan is in control of this world. All unbelievers are enslaved to this world system and under his control. Most will spend their lives fighting an internal battle between what they want to do in their spirit and what they do under the control of the flesh. Some eventually give up. They die inside and become empty and hollow bodies without hope or purpose—the walking dead. It does not need to be so. As children of God we can bring true peace to the warring spirit because of what Jesus did for us. We can help bring peace only if we first have made peace within ourselves.

How do we know if we really have the Peace that passes all understanding? The easiest way might be to look at a life with the absence of that Peace. It is a life of worry—worry about money, jobs, being pretty, being handsome, having a big house or a new car. A life that worries about all the external, worldly things everyone else says are important and valuable. We are to be at Peace. Don't worry!

> Therefore, I say to you, do not worry about your
> life, what you will eat of what you will drink,
> nor about your body, what you will put on. Is
> not life more than food and the body more than
> clothing? (Matthew 6:25).

Let us review: Jesus came to be our Peacemaker. Jesus, God the Son, came to restore harmony between God the Father and man.

Jesus brought peace with Him.

Jesus left His peace with us when He returned to the Father.

Jesus expects to find us in perfect peace upon His return.

Jesus did all this to restore harmony between God and man. The cost of this harmony? It cost Him everything.

It cost Him the loss of His Glory to enter His creation.

It cost Him the humiliation of becoming human.

It cost Him when He restrained His Power to call down legions of angels.

It cost Him the total separation from God the Father when He was on the cross.

It cost Him His death on the cross as the Lamb of God.

Jesus, the God the Son, did it all out of a pure heart with pure love to be the perfect Peacemaker.

The disciple on the journey to become more like the Rabbi must come to the same position. We must have the same relationship with the Father that allows us as children of God to be used to bring that same inner peace to the warring soul of another. We can do this only with pure hearts cleansed and filled with God the Holy Spirit.

We must depart from evil and seek God's peace (Psalms 34:14).

We must let God the Holy Spirit cleanse our hearts so they can be filled with the peace of God.

> But, above all these things put on love, which
> is the bond of perfection. And let the peace of
> God rule in your hearts, to which also you are
> called in one body: and be thankful (Colossians
> 3:14-15).

A heart filled with the peace of God has no room for worldly matters. The world and all of Satan's tricks are filtered through God's Peace and will not touch the disciple (Philippians 4:4-7).

The peace we have through Christ should also be used to maintain peace among God's family as well as the unbeliever (Ephesians 4:3). Factions and "isms" are just ways for Satan to split and neutralize the church.

It is one thing to be at peace with ourselves, but it is another thing to be at peace with the world. We need to be honest and admit it is getting increasingly difficult to be at peace with this world and its people. The truth is we cannot do it as we are. That is why we need to be changed. This is the focus of the journey we are on to become disciples.

Maybe the world is a bit big, for starters. What about our family? Maybe disciples should start by bringing peace to their families.

We have all gone to family reunions. The children are all different, but they are of the same family, all with a common heritage. We may not all get along for long periods of time, but at least we tolerate each other out of respect for our parents. We may not even want to talk to someone, but we manage to survive for the parents. We answer to our parents, not each other!

That all changes if an outsider decides to challenge us. That is when the differences disappear. To the outsider we are one unit, a family! We should have the same approach to the world. We are all children of God. We may have different names, talents, titles, and jobs. We may sing different songs, go to different churches, and worship on different days and in different ways. Those are all worldly distractions. All our actions should be predicated on the same, core position of being children of God, a united army, dispensers of peace and reconciliation to warring spirits in a warring world.

Let us, as disciples of the One and Only Most High God, be a united army radiating the Peace of God to the world.

THOUGHTS TO PONDER

1. Before you can show the Peace of God to others, you must have it yourself. Do you still have a war going on inside you that is robbing you of your peace? Ask God to replace it with His Peace that passes all understanding. It may take a while. Write down your feelings.

2. What changes must take place inside you before you can transmit God's Peace to those around you?

3. What biases must you allow God to remove so you can truly present God's Love to the world?

CHAPTER EIGHT

Blessed are those who are persecuted

Blessed are those who are persecuted for righteousness' sake,
For theirs is the kingdom of heaven. Blessed are you when
they revile and persecute you, and say all kinds of
evil against you falsely for My sake.
—MATTHEW 5:10-11

Here is the stark reality of the life of a disciple of Christ. We will experience the wrath of the world once we become so identified with our Rabbi, the Living Lord.

We will not make it through this step in discipleship if we have not spent the time and effort to allow God to mold us through the previous steps. Did we truly acknowledge our depravity? Did we truly fall before the King of Kings and ask for mercy?

Do we continue to hunger, thirst, and seek after His Word? Are we becoming makers of peace by allowing God the Holy Spirit to rule our lives and filter our sins as reflected by His Mercy? Do we allow God to create in us pure hearts? If not, we are not prepared for the real battle that awaits us.

The disciple of Christ is an easy target for the world. We are a light on a hill, a lamp in the darkness, a foreigner in a strange land. We talk differently. We think differently. We dress differently. We treat others differently. We are easy targets because He was an easy target. We have become like our Master. We become easier to spot the farther we have traveled with our Rabbi, our Master, our Savior, our King.

We should not be surprised. God, through His Holy Word, does not hold back. He makes it very clear the journey while short-lived is not easy. It almost seems He is trying to discourage us at times. The timid of heart need not apply! To enter this journey is to enter a war. It is a spiritual war played out in this physical dimension we call life.

Jesus warns us. He tells us we have a job to do. We are here to spread the news that peace and reconciliation with God is now possible through the atoning work of the cross. He tells us this is the most wonderful news the sinful world absolutely does not want to hear. He tells us He is sending some of us to our deaths. It is not His desire; it is just the price of war. Soldiers get killed in the line of duty (John 15:18-16:4).

> Remember the word that I said to you, A servant is not greater than his master. If they persecuted Me, they will also persecute you. If they kept My word, they will keep yours also (John 15:2).

I can almost understand, speaking from an earthly vantage point, why disciples of Christ are reviled, teased, beaten, and generally mocked. Have you ever traveled to another country? I have. You need permission to enter the country. Normally this means you must carry a passport that identifies you as someone "different." Trust me when I tell you that the normal tourist does not need a passport to let the locals know they do not belong in the country! As much as I tried, I looked different and I acted different. I had different manners of behavior and I talked a different language. I realized as much as I tried to blend in, I stood out. Depending on the times and the country, I was not treated very nicely simply because I was an American. I did not have to do anything. I was not treated nicely for just being.

That is the same for a disciple of Christ. We come to the world of the unsaved as a messenger of Christ. Our passport is God the Holy Spirit within us. We will not be able to make the world like us. We are hated for who we are, not what we do!

Jesus makes it clear that our earthly persecution is the position of highest trust given to disciples. Persecution provides the disciple the largest forum and arena to proclaim the Good News to the unsaved. Jesus even goes so far as to tell us to be prepared for trials because He will provide both the audience and the message we are to give. We will be put on display before the world as examples of everything useless and foolish. Jesus tells us so we will not be afraid. Jesus will provide His Word and His Wisdom to confound and confuse the world. Our previous training, our continued seeking, our continued abiding in Christ will make us willing and able vessels for God the Holy Spirit to use as voices for God's message.

It will be the ultimate expression of our commitment to Christ. It is the final test to show that we have become like our Master, that we are truly a disciple. We will need to respond from a position of controlled strength—not the outer, physical strength of the world but the inner, spiritual strength that comes from an intimate relationship with the Risen Lord. Jesus tells us that by our patience we will possess our souls through these trials (Luke 21:12-19). Our job is to stay firm and endure the battle.

> You therefore must endure hardship as a good
> soldier of Christ (2 Timothy 2:3).

I enlisted in the military, signing a four-year contract, during the Vietnam War. Please understand that to an eighteen-year-old right out of high school, four years sounded like an eternity. I had no idea!

I, like all those in the military, had to go through basic training. It is generally a rather unpleasant experience during which you are emotionally and physically shaken to your core. You are then rebuilt with the character, focus, and inner self-control you will need to fulfill any mission assigned to you.

I was stationed in California during the 1960s. It was not fun being around people who made it very clear with words and hand gestures that they did not appreciate the military, all the time knowing I was defending their right to treat me that way. When my contract, my commitment, was over, I was gone. I had fulfilled my four-year obligation. I was out of there!

It was different a few years later when I returned as an officer. I did not sign a contract; I entered into a commission. I made a covenant, if you will, with the government to serve as long as my country needed me. I tell people I am now retired from active duty, but my commitment remains, the covenant is still in place. I, and all officers like me, can be recalled to active duty at any time. A disciple makes a covenant with his Rabbi, his Master, his Savior. A disciple does not sign a contract. This commission, this covenant, is forever.

A disciple becomes a bondservant of the Lord. A bondservant is someone who willingly chooses to serve his or her master. It is an irrevocable declaration. Mosaic law held that at the end of every seven years, servants were to be given their freedom (Exodus 21:2). If the servant chose to stay, a covenant was made between the servant and the master, and the servant became a bond servant of his master.

> But if the servant plainly says . . . than his master shall bring him to the judges. He shall also bring him to the door, or the doorpost, and his master shall pierce his ear with an awl: and he shall serve him forever (Exodus 21:5-6).

The disciple of Christ is both a soldier and a bondservant; both covenants are forever! Disciples of Christ will be heckled, slandered, beat up, and killed for doing their duty. Disciples of Christ must be single-minded and focused on the mission at hand or they will not be able to complete their tasks. We are reminded that Christ left us His Life as an example.

> Servants, be submissive to your masters with all fear, not only to the good and gentle, but also to the harsh. For this is commendable, if because of conscience toward God one endures grief, suffering wrongfully. For what credit is it if, when you are beaten for your fault, you take it patiently? But when you do good and suffer, if you take it patiently, this is commendable before God. For to this you were called, because Christ also suffered for us, leaving us an example, that you should follow His steps (1 Peter 2:18-21).

We know how Peter felt. He was beaten and jailed for simply telling people the Good News. God intervenes, and Peter rejoices and continues on his mission. Such is war and the life of a soldier (Acts 5:40-41). The story of life is not how often we fall, but how often we get up. How much more so for a disciple?

Things must have gotten so difficult for the first-century church that God needed to remind and encourage its members. God personally intervenes by allowing the Apostle John to have a spiritual peek into the real situation. In Revelation, John is allowed to see the battle, the real players, the ultimate victors, and the vanquished. It is not a pretty picture! It is not for the timid. But like anything else, the greater the cost, the greater the reward!

God reminds us that things will become challenging. Satan is defeated, but the battles will become more and more intense until the war is finished. We will suffer. Some of us will be imprisoned for our faith. Some will be killed in battle (Revelation 2:10). Such is war. But He encourages us to be strong and remain faithful. A crown of life awaits us!

> Do you not know that those who run in a race all run, but one receives the prize? Run in such a way that you may obtain it. And everyone who competes for the prize is temperate in all things. Now they do it to obtain a perishable crown, but we for an imperishable crown (1 Corinthians 9:24-25).

Are you being persecuted right now? Great! You know you are in the battle.

Does life seem to be going along pretty well? Good health? Money in the bank? Get rested! Get prayed up! The time will come when you will be sent back into the battlefield!

THOUGHTS TO PONDER

1. Now is the time to be honest with yourself. You will not make it any further if you have tried to cut corners or have given just lip service to this journey. Now is the time to go back and allow God to complete the previous steps in this life-changing process. What have you continued to hold onto? Give it up now!

2. What does your new relationship with God mean to you?

3. Get ready for an increase in Satan's attacks on you and your loved ones. Keep a log. Keep track of what happens as you respond from a position of strength in Christ.

Rejoice and be exceedingly glad

Rejoice and be exceedingly glad,
for great is your reward in heaven,
for so they persecuted the prophets who were before you.
—MATTHEW 5:12

What a statement, considering what God tells us about the journey planned for His disciples. You are going to be teased, mocked, persecuted, discriminated against, beaten, jailed, and killed for testifying about Christ and His Love. We who live for Christ are always being handed over to die for Jesus' sake (2 Corinthians 4:11).

Rejoice! Have a party! Sing praises to My Name for all that will come about!

Have exceeding joy in your heart. Do not just be happy. Be giddy! Have joy in your heart, a song on your lips, and a bounce to your walk.

Is He serious? How can we do this, you may ask? The same way the apostles did—the same way the martyrs during the Reformation did—just like all the saints before us did. We do it by keeping our eyes on the Author and Finisher of our faith—Christ Jesus! We do it because our Savior waits for us at the finish line. God the Holy Spirit dwells within us, compelling us onward for His Glory. We are no longer our own. Our lives have been absorbed with Christ. We have become and continue to become new creatures in Christ. The physical body is fading away so the spiritual body may grow (2 Corinthians 5:17).

We must remember there can be no victory without first entering the race! We cannot enjoy the destination awaiting us without traveling the road set before us. We cannot cross the finish line without running the race. There are no shortcuts. None!

What rewards is He promising us? Let me list a few:

- A crown of life (James 1:12).

- A place beyond the condemning forces of sin (Romans 8:1).

- A new body (I already have my order in) (Philippians 3:21).

- A place in the New Jerusalem that God had prepared for His children from the beginning of time (Revelation 21:1-2).

- An inheritance that will never end (1 Peter 1:5).

I could go on, but you get the picture. What God has in store for us is awesome!

But that is the end of the journey. What about the journey itself?

Every soldier must go through basic training before being sent off to war; no commanding officer would have it any other way. Can you imagine an untrained and ill-equipped mob going up against a highly trained and disciplined army? It would be a slaughter!

We who have gone through such training know what I am talking about. The trainers break you down so they can build you back up. Each week gets harder and harder because they need to know you are prepared for battle. They need to know you will endure until the end of the mission. They need to know you can be trusted. They need to know you are ready to die if needed.

And we need to know it as well! We need to know the Enemy that waits us. We need to know his power, and we need to know the equipment we have to fight him. We need to know the Power within us is greater than the power in the world.

Graduation day eventually arrives. Soldiers may get a certificate, a new rank, a new beret, or a medal. They will get something to signify they made it! They endured to the end and are now ready for the real mission set before them. Some will survive the many battles. Some will be wounded. Some imprisoned. Some tortured. Some killed. Some will even defect to the other side. All who faithfully complete their assignments will be honored.

Disciples, as members of God's army, look for the same results. Their job is to do their job, to be faithful to our Lord and Master and trust Him with the rest. Paul's last letter we find in the Bible is possibly 2 Timothy. It could be called his last will and testament to the church. Paul encourages the reader to keep pressing on with the Word.

> Preach the word! Be ready in season and out of season. Convince, rebuke, exhort, with all long suffering and teaching. But, you be watchful in all things, endure afflictions, do the work of an evangelist, fulfill your ministry (2 Timothy 4:2-5).

Our journey into discipleship is not an end unto itself. The purpose is not to get a diploma to hang on a wall any more than graduating from basic training is simply to get a certificate or a medal. Completing training is just the start. The disciple is now ready for the real work to begin.

Our mission is to be sent into world so others may know the Truth, so others may know the Love of Christ and believe. Jesus sends us into the world because He knows us. He resides in us.

We disciples can go forth into the world full of joy because we have come so close to our Master, our Rabbi, that we have become like Him. We will bear fruit like Him. We will love like Him. We will love those He loves. We will be hated by those who hate Him. We will be truly free. We will be in the world but no longer enslaved by the world.

> He who loves his life will lose it, and he who hates his life in this world will keep it for eternal life. If anyone serves Me, let him follow Me, and where I am, there My servant will be also. If anyone serves Me, him My Father will honor (John 12:25-26).

Imagine the freedom and joy of being free from the pressures of this world. Imagine not having one care about what other think about you. Imagine the freedom of not needing to wear the best clothes, drive the best car, or spend your life always trying to get that next promotion. Imagine the freedom of simply following the path our Rabbi has set before you without a care as to the outcome. Your mission is simply to fulfill the purpose placed in your heart by God and trusting Him to provide the results according to His Glory.

We will continue to grow as we follow our Master. We will bear more fruit in some years than others. We will be allowed to sit dormant at times so as not to get overworked. And God will prune us so we can grow back stronger and bear even better fruit. But we will always have joy in our heart because we know our Master, our Rabbi, our God!

We will eventually graduate from this physical training ground, our purpose complete. We realize our physical body is worn, tired, and spent. It is getting ready to be discarded so the spiritual body can fly into the arms of our Savior. I am convinced that no one or no thing will be allowed to shorten our stay on this earth until our mission is done. I am also sure God does not allow us to linger to long afterward. What would be the point?

It may sound like the disciple has "given up" all the thing of the flesh. In reality, the disciple has just "given back" to Christ the life He has given us though His atoning work on the cross.

Truly we are not giving up that much. Anyone who can divide two numbers understands what I mean. We give back to God sixty, seventy, eighty, or ninety years in exchange for eternity. Now I do not know how you calculate it, but ninety years divided by eternity is a mighty small number! Paul calls this life "temporary" (2 Corinthians 4:18). I call it even less than that! In terms of today's vernacular, it is far less than a nanosecond!

It is essentially nothing! Life shrinks to nothing in the face of eternity. That is worth repeating: this life fades into nothingness in the face of eternity!

What awaits us? Our Master and Lord, Christ Jesus. He will wipe away any lingering tears. He will wrap us in His loving arms. We will weep for joy. We have overcome the world! We will experience pure love and peace—and be at rest!

> Therefore you now have sorrow but I will see you again and your heart will rejoice, and your joy no one will take from you (John 16:22).

Only an all-powerful, all-loving God can make that kind of promise. We can rejoice because He has prepared the way. We will shed this physical body for a beautiful, spiritual body. He is promising us it will be alright.

One last thought—what will be the footnote at the end of your life? What will be on your headstone? What will summarize your journey through this world? Here is a suggestion:

> I have glorified You on earth. I have finished the work which You have given Me to do (John 17:4).

Jesus overcame the world! So have you in Christ our Lord!

Do we have a reason to rejoice and be glad? Do we have a reason to jump and shout with joy? I think so! One journey will be over. Another one will only be starting.

What a glorious day that will be!

CHAPTER NINE

THOUGHTS TO PONDER

1. Are you prepared for the battles ahead? If not, what do you
    need to do to become "battle ready"?

2. What past experiences do you now see as God's way of
    preparing you for what may lie ahead? What has been your
    "basic training" experience?

3. How will this new perspective on the rewards ahead change
    how you will approach the day? How you interact with
    others?

CHAPTER TEN

Conclusion: Are you ready?

R.DISPAIN '12

You are the light of the world. A city that is set on a hill cannot
be hidden. Let your light so shine before men, that they may
see your good works and glorify your Father in heaven
(MATTHEW 5:14, 16).

No one can obtain a victory without engaging in a battle. No one
should enter into a battle without being prepared, committed,
and knowledgeable of the cost. You are now disciples of the
Most High God. You are God's Light to the world.

You reached the end of the line and surrendered to God. You
confessed your sinful condition, and your spirit is renewed with
the Spirit of God. You experienced the remorse of your actions
and have felt the warmth and comfort of God's Grace. You now

continuously seek and enjoy the righteousness from God. You can now show and reflect God's Mercy, having experienced it yourself. You can now act out of a pure heart, with pure motives, to offer God's Peace to the troubled spirits around you. You are a new creature, a disciple who knows the battles that await. Your right standing with God places you in wrong standing with the world. You are now so identified with Christ that others see Him when they look at you! The world hates you because it hates Him!

No leader would send into battle troops who lack the knowledge, training, and equipment needed to sustain them in battle. No leader would commit troops to battle without counting the cost. The cost is great; it cost our Lord His death on the cross.

God the Father provides the strength (the Holy Sprit), the armor, the training, and the mission. We are well prepared for the war ahead. There will be many battles, but we know the outcome. We have been given the end of the story. It reads like this:

> What then shall we say to these things? If God is
> for us, who can be against us? (Romans 8:31).

Disciples of God are lights in the darkness reflecting the Light that is within them. God the Father, through God the Son, fills us through God the Holy Spirit to spread His message to the world. We have put on the armor of Light. We have put on Christ!

> The night is far spent, the day is at hand.
> Therefore let us cast off the works of darkness,
> and let us put on the armor of light. Let us
> walk properly, as in the day, not in revelry and
> drunkenness, not in lewdness and lust, not
> in strife and envy. But put on the Lord Jesus

Christ, and make no provision for the flesh, to
fulfill its lust (Romans 13:12-14).

Make no mistake! The world of the unsaved is one of darkness.
Their thoughts are empty, their lives are empty, and their spirits
are empty. They grope after and follow anything and anyone
who promises to give them direction. They follow the latest
philosophy, the latest path to enlightenment, or the latest feel-
good fad. They will "suck it out" or "fill it in" just to make
themselves feel and look good. They are like people in a dark
cave without light. They stumble around hunting for a way out.
Paul puts it this way:

> . . . because, although they knew God, they did
> not glorify Him as God; nor were thankful, but
> became futile in their thoughts, and their foolish
> hearts were darkened (Romans 1:21).

Disciples of the Most High God are the only guides with the
only Light that will get the unsaved out of the cave. The disciples
are the mirrors in the lighthouse that will allow God's Love to
shine into the unrighteousness of the souls of the unsaved. They
know what they need; it is just buried deep within them. Those
who are unsaved do not want to face what they know to be true,
so they hang around with others just like themselves.

> Who, knowing the righteous judgment of God,
> that those who practice such things are deserving
> of death, not only do the same, but also approve
> of those who practice them (Romans 1:32).

I call this the "messy closet" syndrome. You know what I am
talking about. Everyone has one. Mine is in my office. Anything
without a place in the house gets shoved into a closet, never to
been seen again. It starts out innocently enough—a little here,
a little there. As time goes by, that closet becomes dark and

sinister. It has reached the point that fear and dread hang over my wife and me every time we go into that closet. We don't really know everything that is in the closet; we just know it is best not to go there. The same is true with the deep recesses of the souls of the unsaved! They know some ugly things are deep down within them. They know, somewhere deep in their memory, they will need to face all the ugliness someday. They just choose to do all they can to avoid it now!

The Light within us is the only thing that can penetrate deep enough to save them. It is painful on their part and dangerous on our part. It is a spiritual war. The Enemy will not give up easily. Satan wants to keep them in darkness because they cannot deal with what is kept in darkness, and they cannot deal with what they cannot see. They cannot deal with what they do not acknowledge to exist.

Jesus, our Master and Savior, is very clear about the Enemy, the challenge, the cost, and the reward. We will obtain victory only if we follow the course set before us. It is clear; it is the road He traveled. He promises the victory ahead of us is worth the path forged and fought behind us!

Does He really expect us to travel the same road? Yes! Why? Because that is what it means to be a disciple of Christ and identify with Him. Who better to help guide those in darkness than those who were in the same dark cave once themselves? We can relate! Most will stay in the darkness, but some will follow the Light! We have committed ourselves to becoming like our Rabbi so we can reflect that Light.

The unsaved are in bondage. Their spirits are overcome with the sense of defeat, remorse, and loss of hope that results from the darkness of a sin-sick soul. Disciples bring hope and light into their lives become they can show the unsaved how to overcome their hopeless lives because disciples have overcome the same thing.

> You are of God, little children, and have overcome
> them, because He who is in you is greater than
> he who is in the world (1 John 4:4).

The Light, or Presence of God, once resided only in the earthly temple. Believers were required to travel to the temple to worship and hope to feel the Presence of the Living God. Jesus changed that when He died on the cross. The veil that separated God from the people was torn down. We became the temples of God. We are filled with the Spirit of God to spread His Glory.

> Do you not know that you are the temple of
> God and that the Spirit of God dwells in you?
> If anyone defiles the temple of God, God will
> destroy him. For the temple of God is Holy,
> which temple you are (1 Corinthians 3:16-17).

Now we can fully understand the importance of this process Jesus speaks about in what we call the Beatitudes. This is not a position to be taken lightly.

I know if you are like me, you are wondering whether you are up to the task. We are disciples of Christ, but we are not Christ. Maybe God could find someone better for this responsibility? Someone with a brighter light? Do not doubt your abilities; God is never wrong.

A lighthouse is always built on solid rock so it can weather the strongest storms. A lighthouse is built to show those in the storm the way to safety. The outside may get beaten and worn, but the inside is secure with the light needed to show the way. We are His lighthouses. We each have the same Light within us, but some of us have just been cleaning our mirrors longer than others. Remember the light in the cave. Its impact depends on not only the brightness of the light but the darkness of the cave. The Light you send out can penetrate the deepest darkness of the soul.

Waves of light, unlike sound waves, are more focused. They are like the stones used by David. You remember the story in 1 Samuel 17. David selected smooth stones with which to go after Goliath, and he took five of them not out of lack of faith but because Goliath had brothers! David was single-minded and focused. He knew how to direct his stone at his target. He did not just throw it up and hope it would hit Goliath. David had a specific target in mind, and your light is being specifically directed at the people around you. Let God the Holy Spirit direct you to the targets of His Light. Your life with be the light that draws them, and the words you speak will be as focused and effective as David's stones, both being directed by God.

Many of us are just getting out of basic training. The operative word is "basic." We will continue to clean our mirrors as time goes on to allow the Light of the Lord to shine more brightly into the dark world. Our mirrors (our bodies) will get beat up and scratched. They will constantly need to be cleaned after battle, and they will get worn and worn out. But the Light—the Light will grow brighter and brighter as time marches on. Our job is to do our job and glorify God each step of the way.

I heard it said once that our best day on earth cannot compare to what awaits us in heaven. The absolutely worst, most painful, and most horrible day on earth for the unbeliever cannot compare to the judgment that awaits in the eternity of hell. What awaits us in heaven can get only better; what awaits us in hell can get only worse!

God's Word spoke light into the darkness of the newly created physical world. Jesus brought the Light of God's Grace and Mercy into the spiritual darkness of this world. God sends the disciple out with His Light, hoping to show those in darkness the way to the Light. The stakes are high with eternal consequences.

Eventually, our lives will be spent physically, emotionally, and spiritually. It happened to Jesus on the cross, and it will happen to us. Jesus despised the shame of the cross, knowing the Glory of the Father that waited for Him. We should remember we are disciples; we will endure because He endured. We will rejoice because He rejoiced (Hebrews 12:1-4).

The glory of the law brought a glory that only faded, but the Glory of God, brought by Jesus through the Holy Spirit, lasts forever. We bring the light of God's Glory that will not fade! That is the message we bring to the world! We are the messengers, the letters of God to the world. The veil of the temple is torn in two. All who wish may enter into the Presence of God.

It is now finished. We know the conditions of discipleship: its path, its cost, and its reward. I started out by saying we have really only one choice in life—to choose our master!

> And if it seems evil to you to serve the Lord, choose for yourselves this day whom you will serve, whether the gods which your fathers served that were on the other side of the River. Or the gods of the Amorites, in whose land you dwell. But as for me and my house, we will serve the Lord (Joshua 24:15).

Me? I will be happy if the first words I hear after the last breath I take are, "Welcome Home!"

Enjoy the journey!

Afterword

The Bible has some great prayers. A number of years ago I decided to personalize the prayer found in Ephesians 3:14-21. It gets me started for the day, and I hope it does the same for you.

Father, I come and bow down before you through our Lord, Christ Jesus, in Whom the whole family of God, in heaven and on earth, is named. I pray that You would grant me, according to the riches of Your Glory, to be strengthened today with Your mighty power through Your Holy Spirit that dwells within me. I pray that Christ may dwell in my heart through faith, that I may be rooted and grounded in our love, and that I may be able to comprehend the width and length and depth and height of Your Love. I pray that I may know the Love of Christ, which passes all my knowledge and understanding, and that I will be filled with all Your Blessings and Wisdom. Now to You, Most High God, Who is able to do exceedingly abundantly above all that I could ever ask or think, according to Your great and awesome power that works within me, be all glory through Christ Jesus forever and ever, Amen.

Acknowledgement

I would like to thank my brother, Robert {Rob) R. D'Spain for the wonderful artwork seen throughout the book. Rob is a free lance illustrator and lives in the San Francisco Bay area of California. Best known for his artistic renderings of commercial buildings, he is a superb artist and works in several mediums. His contribution to this book is priceless. It is my hope that the emotions evoked by the images will open a door for reflection and meditation.

About The Author

Michael D'Spain has been a licensed minister for over thirty years through Fuller Life Fellowship. While never called into full-time ministry, he has acted in numerous lay positions throughout the years. He has spoken to groups, and he leads Bible studies in the United States and Europe.

Michael has been active in community events, helping to spread the gospel as the Lord provided. He has spoken at citywide prayer events and was one of the main speakers at the Montana governor's annual prayer breakfast.

Michael is a retired military officer. He has been married to Gail for over forty years, and they have three grown boys.

This is Michael's first book as the Lord leads him into a new phase of his ministry.

He can be reached at mldspain@gmail.com.

Printed in the United States
By Bookmasters